Zauberhafte Geschichten in Englisch und Deutsch: Zweisprachige Abenteuer für Kinder

Artici English

Published by Artici English, 2024.

ZAUBERHAFTE GESCHICHTEN IN ENGLISCH UND DEUTSCH: ZWEISPRACHIGE ABENTEUER FÜR KINDER

First edition. June 3, 2024.

ISBN: 979-8227067357

Written by Artici English.

Table of Contents

The Marvelous Mermaid Adventure

In the deepest part of the ocean, where the water shimmered with a thousand shades of blue, lived a young mermaid named Marissa. Marissa wasn't just any mermaid; she was the most curious and adventurous mermaid in the entire ocean. With her long, flowing hair the color of seaweed and eyes as bright as the morning sun, she was always eager to explore the mysteries of the sea.

One sunny day, as Marissa swam near the coral reef, she discovered a sparkling seashell unlike any she had ever seen. It glowed with an enchanting light, and as she picked it up, she heard a faint whisper, "Help me, please!"

Startled, Marissa looked around but saw no one. The voice seemed to be coming from the seashell itself. "Who are you?" Marissa asked, her heart pounding with excitement.

"I am Princess Marina," the voice replied. "I've been trapped in this shell by an evil sea witch. Only someone with a brave heart can set me free."

Without a second thought, Marissa vowed to help the princess. She knew the journey ahead would be dangerous, but her adventurous spirit could not be tamed.

Marissa swam through dark underwater caves and past giant sea creatures. She faced fierce storms and outsmarted tricky sea urchins. Her bravery and quick thinking guided her through every challenge. Along the way, she met a quirky seahorse named Sammy, who decided to join her on her quest.

Sammy was a funny little fellow with a knack for getting into trouble. He made Marissa laugh with his silly antics and kept her spirits high even in the scariest moments. Together, they made a great team.

Finally, they reached the lair of the evil sea witch. The lair was surrounded by swirling whirlpools and guarded by sharp-toothed eels. Marissa's heart raced, but she knew she couldn't turn back now.

With a deep breath, Marissa and Sammy sneaked into the lair. They found the sea witch cackling over a cauldron filled with a bubbling potion. The witch was tall and menacing, with long, twisted hair and a wicked grin.

"Who dares to enter my lair?" the sea witch hissed.

Marissa stepped forward, her voice steady. "I am Marissa, and I've come to set Princess Marina free."

The sea witch laughed, a sound like nails on a chalkboard. "You think you can defeat me, little mermaid? Very well, let's see if you have the courage."

With a wave of her hand, the sea witch conjured a massive wave to wash Marissa and Sammy away. But Marissa remembered the glowing seashell and held it up high. The shell emitted a bright light that repelled the wave and sent the sea witch stumbling backward.

Enraged, the sea witch cast a spell to turn Marissa into stone. But Sammy, with his quick thinking, splashed water from the cauldron onto the witch. The potion reversed the witch's spell, and she turned into a harmless sea cucumber.

With the sea witch defeated, the seashell glowed even brighter. Marissa carefully opened it, and in a burst of light, Princess Marina emerged, free at last. She was beautiful, with flowing hair and a shimmering tail.

"Thank you, Marissa," the princess said, her eyes sparkling with gratitude. "You have shown great courage and kindness."

As a reward, Princess Marina granted Marissa and Sammy three wishes. Marissa wished for all the sea creatures to live in peace, for Sammy to have endless adventures, and for herself to continue exploring the wonders of the ocean.

And so, Marissa and Sammy returned home as heroes, celebrated by all the creatures of the sea. They continued to have many more marvelous adventures, always guided by their bravery and friendship.

And every time Marissa looked at the shimmering seashell, she remembered that no challenge was too great when faced with a brave heart and a true friend by her side.

Das Wunderbare Abenteuer der Meerjungfrau

In den tiefsten Teilen des Ozeans, wo das Wasser in tausend Blautönen schimmerte, lebte eine junge Meerjungfrau namens Marissa. Marissa war nicht nur irgendeine Meerjungfrau; sie war die neugierigste und abenteuerlustigste Meerjungfrau im ganzen Ozean. Mit ihren langen, fließenden Haaren in der Farbe von Seetang und Augen so hell wie die Morgensonne, war sie immer bereit, die Geheimnisse des Meeres zu erkunden.

Eines sonnigen Tages, als Marissa in der Nähe des Korallenriffs schwamm, entdeckte sie eine funkelnde Muschel, wie sie noch nie eine gesehen hatte. Sie glühte mit einem verzaubernden Licht, und als sie sie aufhob, hörte sie ein leises Flüstern: "Hilf mir, bitte!"

Erschrocken schaute sich Marissa um, aber sie sah niemanden. Die Stimme schien direkt aus der Muschel zu kommen. "Wer bist du?" fragte Marissa, ihr Herz vor Aufregung klopfend.

"Ich bin Prinzessin Marina," antwortete die Stimme. "Ich wurde von einer bösen Meereshexe in diese Muschel eingesperrt. Nur jemand mit einem tapferen Herzen kann mich befreien."

Ohne zu zögern versprach Marissa, der Prinzessin zu helfen. Sie wusste, dass die Reise gefährlich sein würde, aber ihr abenteuerlicher Geist ließ sich nicht zähmen.

Marissa schwamm durch dunkle Unterwasserhöhlen und an riesigen Meeresbewohnern vorbei. Sie stellte sich wilden Stürmen und überlistete trickreiche Seeigel. Ihr Mut und ihr schnelles Denken führten sie durch jede Herausforderung. Unterwegs traf sie ein quirliges Seepferdchen namens Sammy, das beschloss, sich ihrer Mission anzuschließen.

Sammy war ein lustiger kleiner Kerl, der ständig in Schwierigkeiten geriet. Er brachte Marissa mit seinen albernen Streichen zum Lachen und hielt ihre Laune auch in den gruseligsten Momenten hoch. Zusammen waren sie ein großartiges Team.

Schließlich erreichten sie das Versteck der bösen Meereshexe. Das Versteck war von wirbelnden Strudeln umgeben und wurde von scharfzähnigen Aalen bewacht. Marissas Herz raste, aber sie wusste, dass sie jetzt nicht mehr umkehren konnte.

Mit einem tiefen Atemzug schlichen sich Marissa und Sammy in das Versteck. Sie fanden die Meereshexe kichernd über einem Kessel mit einer brodelnden Flüssigkeit. Die Hexe war groß und bedrohlich, mit langen, verdrehten Haaren und einem bösen Grinsen.

"Wer wagt es, mein Versteck zu betreten?" zischte die Meereshexe.

Marissa trat vor, ihre Stimme fest. "Ich bin Marissa, und ich bin hier, um Prinzessin Marina zu befreien."

Die Meereshexe lachte, ein Geräusch wie Nägel auf einer Tafel. "Du denkst, du kannst mich besiegen, kleine Meerjungfrau? Sehr gut, lass uns sehen, ob du den Mut hast."

Mit einer Handbewegung rief die Meereshexe eine riesige Welle herbei, um Marissa und Sammy fortzuspülen. Doch Marissa erinnerte sich an die funkelnde Muschel und hielt sie hoch. Die Muschel strahlte ein helles Licht aus, das die Welle abwehrte und die Meereshexe zurückstolpern ließ.

Wütend sprach die Meereshexe einen Zauber, um Marissa in Stein zu verwandeln. Doch Sammy, mit seinem schnellen Denken, spritzte Wasser aus dem Kessel auf die Hexe. Der Trank kehrte den Zauber der Hexe um, und sie verwandelte sich in eine harmlose Seegurke.

Mit der besiegten Meereshexe leuchtete die Muschel noch heller. Marissa öffnete sie vorsichtig, und in einem Lichtblitz erschien Prinzessin Marina, endlich befreit. Sie war wunderschön, mit fließendem Haar und einem schimmernden Schwanz.

"Danke, Marissa," sagte die Prinzessin, ihre Augen funkelten vor Dankbarkeit. "Du hast großen Mut und Freundlichkeit gezeigt."

Als Belohnung gewährte Prinzessin Marina Marissa und Sammy drei Wünsche. Marissa wünschte sich, dass alle Meeresbewohner in Frieden leben könnten, dass Sammy endlose Abenteuer erleben würde, und dass sie selbst weiterhin die Wunder des Ozeans erkunden könnte.

Und so kehrten Marissa und Sammy als Helden nach Hause zurück, gefeiert von allen Kreaturen des Meeres. Sie erlebten weiterhin viele wunderbare Abenteuer, immer geleitet von ihrem Mut und ihrer Freundschaft.

Und jedes Mal, wenn Marissa die funkelnde Muschel ansah, erinnerte sie sich daran, dass keine Herausforderung zu groß war, wenn man ein tapferes Herz und einen wahren Freund an seiner Seite hatte.

The Daring Dragon and the Incredible Adventure

In a faraway kingdom, nestled between rolling green hills and misty forests, there was a bustling village called Little Wisp. Little Wisp was famous for two things: its delicious pastries and the legend of a dragon named Duncan. Duncan wasn't just any dragon; he was the smallest dragon in the land, with emerald-green scales and wings that sparkled in the sunlight. Duncan loved to explore, but his tiny size made it hard for others to take him seriously.

One day, as the villagers prepared for their annual festival, an alarming news spread through Little Wisp. The town's most treasured artifact, the Golden Acorn, had been stolen by a mischievous wizard named Zoltar. The Golden Acorn was said to bring prosperity to the village, and without it, Little Wisp was sure to fall into hard times.

The villagers were in despair. They knew that Zoltar lived in a towering castle on the highest peak of the Forbidden Mountains, a place filled with dangers and dark magic. No one dared to embark on such a perilous journey, except for one brave little dragon.

Duncan, hearing the cries of the villagers, decided it was his time to shine. "I will retrieve the Golden Acorn!" he declared, his voice filled with determination.

The villagers were skeptical. "You're too small, Duncan," they said. "The Forbidden Mountains are too dangerous for you."

But Duncan was resolute. He spread his shimmering wings and took off towards the Forbidden Mountains, his heart filled with courage.

The journey was treacherous. Duncan flew over deep valleys and dense forests, facing fierce winds and icy snowstorms. He encountered towering cliffs and had to navigate through mazes of thorny bushes. Despite the challenges, Duncan pressed on, his eyes set on the distant peak where Zoltar's castle stood.

On his way, Duncan met a clever fox named Felix. Felix had a reputation for being cunning and resourceful. "Where are you heading, little dragon?" Felix asked, his eyes twinkling with curiosity.

"I'm going to retrieve the Golden Acorn from Zoltar's castle," Duncan replied bravely.

Felix was impressed by Duncan's courage. "You'll need my help," he said. "I know the way through the mountains, and together, we can outsmart Zoltar."

And so, Duncan and Felix became a team. They faced many obstacles together, from tricksy trolls to swirling whirlpools. Felix's cunning tricks and Duncan's fiery breath helped them overcome every challenge.

When they finally reached Zoltar's castle, they were met with a formidable sight. The castle was surrounded by a moat of boiling lava and guarded by fire-breathing gargoyles. Duncan's heart pounded, but he remembered the villagers counting on him.

"Leave this to me," Felix whispered. He devised a clever plan to distract the gargoyles while Duncan slipped inside the castle.

Inside, the castle was dark and eerie. Duncan tiptoed through the shadowy halls, his scales reflecting the flickering torchlight. At last, he found the Golden Acorn, glowing softly on a pedestal. But just as he reached out to grab it, Zoltar appeared in a puff of smoke.

"So, the tiny dragon has come to steal my treasure," Zoltar sneered. "You'll never succeed!"

Duncan stood his ground. "I'm not afraid of you, Zoltar. The Golden Acorn belongs to the people of Little Wisp, and I'm taking it back."

With a burst of courage, Duncan breathed a stream of fire at Zoltar. The wizard dodged, but in his haste, he knocked over a shelf of potions. Colorful liquids spilled everywhere, causing a magical explosion that sent Zoltar flying out of the window, shrieking as he disappeared into the distance.

Duncan grabbed the Golden Acorn and hurried out of the castle, reuniting with Felix. Together, they flew back to Little Wisp, the precious artifact safe in Duncan's claws.

When Duncan and Felix returned to the village, they were greeted with cheers and joyous celebrations. The villagers couldn't believe their eyes. "You did it, Duncan!" they cried. "You brought back the Golden Acorn!"

From that day on, Duncan was no longer seen as the smallest dragon, but as the bravest. He had proven that size didn't matter when it came to courage and determination. Little Wisp flourished once more, thanks to Duncan and his daring adventure.

Duncan and Felix continued to have many more incredible adventures, always ready to help those in need. And every year, during the festival, the villagers would tell the story of the tiny dragon who saved their village, inspiring everyone to believe in their own bravery and strength.

Der Kühne Drache und das Unglaubliche Abenteuer

In einem weit entfernten Königreich, eingebettet zwischen sanften grünen Hügeln und nebligen Wäldern, lag ein lebhaftes Dorf namens Kleines Flimmerlicht. Kleines Flimmerlicht war bekannt für zwei Dinge: seine köstlichen Gebäcke und die Legende eines Drachens namens Duncan. Duncan war nicht einfach irgendein Drache; er war der kleinste Drache im Land, mit smaragdgrünen Schuppen und Flügeln, die im Sonnenlicht funkelten. Duncan liebte es zu erkunden, aber seine winzige Größe machte es anderen schwer, ihn ernst zu nehmen.

Eines Tages, als die Dorfbewohner sich auf ihr jährliches Fest vorbereiteten, verbreitete sich eine alarmierende Nachricht durch Kleines Flimmerlicht. Das kostbarste Artefakt der Stadt, die Goldene Eichel, war von einem schelmischen Zauberer namens Zoltar gestohlen worden. Die Goldene Eichel sollte Wohlstand in das Dorf bringen, und ohne sie würde Kleines Flimmerlicht sicherlich harte Zeiten erleben.

Die Dorfbewohner waren verzweifelt. Sie wussten, dass Zoltar in einem hoch aufragenden Schloss auf dem höchsten Gipfel der Verbotenen Berge lebte, einem Ort voller Gefahren und dunkler Magie. Niemand wagte es, sich auf eine so gefährliche Reise zu begeben, außer einem tapferen kleinen Drachen.

Duncan, der die Rufe der Dorfbewohner hörte, beschloss, dass jetzt seine Zeit gekommen war, sich zu beweisen. "Ich werde die Goldene Eichel zurückholen!" erklärte er, seine Stimme voller Entschlossenheit.

Die Dorfbewohner waren skeptisch. "Du bist zu klein, Duncan", sagten sie. "Die Verbotenen Berge sind zu gefährlich für dich."

Aber Duncan war unerschütterlich. Er breitete seine schimmernden Flügel aus und flog in Richtung der Verbotenen Berge, sein Herz erfüllt von Mut.

Die Reise war gefährlich. Duncan flog über tiefe Täler und dichte Wälder, trotzte heftigen Winden und eisigen Schneestürmen. Er traf auf hohe Klippen und musste sich durch Irrgärten von Dornenbüschen navigieren. Trotz der Herausforderungen drängte Duncan weiter, seine Augen auf den fernen Gipfel gerichtet, auf dem Zoltars Schloss stand.

Auf seinem Weg traf Duncan einen cleveren Fuchs namens Felix. Felix hatte den Ruf, schlau und einfallsreich zu sein. "Wohin gehst du, kleiner Drache?" fragte Felix, seine Augen vor Neugier funkelnd.

"Ich werde die Goldene Eichel aus Zoltars Schloss holen", antwortete Duncan tapfer.

Felix war beeindruckt von Duncans Mut. "Du wirst meine Hilfe brauchen", sagte er. "Ich kenne den Weg durch die Berge, und zusammen können wir Zoltar überlisten."

Und so wurden Duncan und Felix ein Team. Sie meisterten viele Hindernisse gemeinsam, von listigen Trollen bis hin zu wirbelnden Strudeln. Felix' clevere Tricks und Duncans feuriger Atem halfen ihnen, jede Herausforderung zu überwinden.

Als sie schließlich Zoltars Schloss erreichten, wurden sie mit einem imposanten Anblick konfrontiert. Das Schloss war von einem Graben aus brodelnder Lava umgeben und von feuerspeienden Gargoyles bewacht. Duncans Herz schlug schneller, aber er erinnerte sich an die Dorfbewohner, die auf ihn zählten.

"Überlass das mir", flüsterte Felix. Er entwickelte einen cleveren Plan, um die Gargoyles abzulenken, während Duncan ins Schloss schlüpfte.

Im Inneren war das Schloss dunkel und unheimlich. Duncan schlich durch die schattigen Gänge, seine Schuppen spiegelten das flackernde Fackellicht wider. Schließlich fand er die Goldene Eichel, die sanft auf einem Podest glühte. Doch gerade als er danach griff, erschien Zoltar in einer Rauchwolke.

"Also, der winzige Drache ist gekommen, um meinen Schatz zu stehlen", spottete Zoltar. "Du wirst niemals Erfolg haben!"

Duncan blieb standhaft. "Ich habe keine Angst vor dir, Zoltar. Die Goldene Eichel gehört den Menschen von Kleines Flimmerlicht, und ich nehme sie zurück."

Mit einem plötzlichen Mutstoß spie Duncan einen Feuerstrahl auf Zoltar. Der Zauberer wich aus, aber in seiner Hast stieß er ein Regal mit Tränken um. Farbige Flüssigkeiten ergossen sich überall und verursachten eine magische Explosion, die Zoltar aus dem Fenster schleuderte, während er in die Ferne schrie und verschwand.

Duncan schnappte sich die Goldene Eichel und eilte aus dem Schloss, wo er sich mit Felix wieder vereinte. Zusammen flogen sie zurück nach Kleines Flimmerlicht, das kostbare Artefakt sicher in Duncans Krallen.

Als Duncan und Felix ins Dorf zurückkehrten, wurden sie mit Jubel und fröhlichen Feierlichkeiten begrüßt. Die Dorfbewohner konnten ihren Augen nicht trauen. "Du hast es geschafft, Duncan!" riefen sie. "Du hast die Goldene Eichel zurückgebracht!"

Von diesem Tag an wurde Duncan nicht mehr als der kleinste Drache angesehen, sondern als der tapferste. Er hatte bewiesen, dass Größe keine Rolle spielt, wenn es um Mut und Entschlossenheit geht. Kleines Flimmerlicht blühte dank Duncan und seinem kühnen Abenteuer wieder auf.

Duncan und Felix erlebten viele weitere unglaubliche Abenteuer, immer bereit, denen zu helfen, die Hilfe brauchten. Und jedes Jahr, während des Festes, erzählten die Dorfbewohner die Geschichte des winzigen Drachen, der ihr Dorf gerettet hatte, und inspirierten jeden dazu, an seine eigene Tapferkeit und Stärke zu glauben.

Farmer Frank's Fantastic Farm

Once upon a time, in a quaint little village called Willowbrook, there lived a farmer named Frank. Farmer Frank was a jolly fellow, with a round belly, a big bushy beard, and a pair of sparkling eyes that always seemed to be twinkling with mischief. His farm, which lay just on the outskirts of the village, was unlike any other. It was a magical place where the most extraordinary things happened.

You see, Farmer Frank's farm was home to a variety of unusual animals. There was Bella, the cow who could jump over the moon; Max, the sheep who could knit his own wool into cozy sweaters; and Chester, the pig who could paint beautiful pictures with his curly tail. But the most remarkable of all was a chicken named Henrietta, who laid golden eggs.

Every morning, the villagers would gather at the farm to see what new marvels awaited them. Children would giggle in delight as Bella performed her moon jumps, and they would watch in awe as Max knitted scarves and hats for everyone. Chester's paintings were so exquisite that they were displayed in the village hall for all to admire. And, of course, everyone marveled at Henrietta's golden eggs, which were said to bring good luck to anyone who found one.

One bright and sunny day, a strange letter arrived for Farmer Frank. It was sealed with a golden crest and looked very important. Frank opened it with curiosity and read aloud:

Frank's eyes lit up with excitement. "This is our chance, everyone!" he exclaimed to his animals. "We'll show the world just how fantastic our farm is!"

The animals cheered, each eager to play their part. They spent the next few weeks practicing and perfecting their acts. Bella honed her moon-jumping skills, Max knitted faster than ever, Chester painted a masterpiece, and Henrietta laid her most dazzling golden eggs.

The day of the Great Village Fair arrived, and the atmosphere was buzzing with excitement. Farmers from near and far had brought their finest animals, each hoping to win the grand prize. The fairground was filled with stalls, games, and delicious food, and the air was filled with the sounds of laughter and music.

When it was Farmer Frank's turn to showcase his animals, the crowd watched in anticipation. Bella began with her spectacular moon jumps, soaring high into the sky and landing gracefully to the cheers of the audience. Max followed, knitting an enormous blanket in record time, his nimble hooves working like magic.

Chester then unveiled his painting, a breathtaking landscape that left everyone speechless. Finally, Henrietta strutted onto the stage and laid a golden egg, which sparkled brilliantly in the sunlight.

The judges, including the distinguished Lord Pompington himself, were thoroughly impressed. They whispered among themselves, nodding and smiling as they deliberated. At last, Lord Pompington stood up and announced, "The winner of the Great Village Fair, and the title of 'Best Farmer in the Land,' is none other than Farmer Frank and his fantastic animals!"

The crowd erupted in applause, and Frank's animals jumped and danced with joy. Frank beamed with pride as he accepted the grand prize, thanking the judges and the villagers for their support. He knew that it was not just his animals' talents that had won the day, but also the love and care they all shared.

From that day on, Farmer Frank's farm became even more famous, attracting visitors from all over who wanted to see the magical animals. Frank used the prize money to improve the farm, making it an even better place for his beloved animals. He built a new barn for Bella, a knitting studio for Max, an art gallery for Chester, and a golden nest for Henrietta.

But the best part of it all was the bond that grew even stronger between Frank and his animals. They continued to amaze and delight the villagers with their extraordinary talents, and their friendship blossomed with each passing day. Together, they showed that with a little bit of magic and a lot of heart, anything is possible.

Bauer Franks Fantastischer Bauernhof

Es war einmal in einem malerischen kleinen Dorf namens Weidenbach ein Bauer namens Frank. Bauer Frank war ein fröhlicher Geselle mit einem runden Bauch, einem großen buschigen Bart und einem Paar funkelnder Augen, die immer zu voller Schabernack zu glänzen schienen. Sein Hof, der direkt am Rande des Dorfes lag, war anders als jeder andere. Es war ein magischer Ort, an dem die außergewöhnlichsten Dinge geschahen.

Sie sehen, Bauernhof von Bauer Frank war die Heimat einer Vielzahl ungewöhnlicher Tiere. Da war Bella, die Kuh, die über den Mond springen konnte; Max, das Schaf, das seine eigene Wolle zu gemütlichen Pullovern stricken konnte; und Chester, das Schwein, das mit seinem lockigen Schwanz wunderschöne Bilder malen konnte. Aber das bemerkenswerteste von allem war ein Huhn namens Henrietta, das goldene Eier legte.

Jeden Morgen versammelten sich die Dorfbewohner auf dem Hof, um zu sehen, welche neuen Wunder auf sie warteten. Die Kinder kicherten vor Freude, wenn Bella ihre Mondsprünge machte, und sie schauten mit Ehrfurcht, wie Max Schals und Hüte für alle strickte. Chesters Gemälde waren so exquisit, dass sie im Gemeindehaus ausgestellt wurden, damit alle sie bewundern konnten. Und natürlich staunte jeder über

Henriettas goldene Eier, von denen gesagt wurde, dass sie jedem Glück bringen, der eins fand.

An einem hellen und sonnigen Tag kam ein seltsamer Brief für Bauer Frank an. Er war mit einem goldenen Wappen versiegelt und sah sehr wichtig aus. Frank öffnete ihn neugierig und las laut vor:

Lieber Bauer Frank,

Sie sind herzlich eingeladen, am Großen Dorffest teilzunehmen, bei dem Bauern aus der ganzen Umgebung antreten werden, um die außergewöhnlichsten Talente ihrer Tiere zu präsentieren. Der Gewinner erhält einen großen Preis von 1000 Goldmünzen und den angesehenen Titel 'Bester Bauer des Landes'.

Mit freundlichen Grüßen,

Lord Pompington

Franks Augen leuchteten vor Aufregung. "Das ist unsere Chance, Leute!" rief er seinen Tieren zu. "Wir werden der Welt zeigen, wie fantastisch unser Hof ist!"

Die Tiere jubelten, jeder von ihnen begierig, seinen Teil beizutragen. Sie verbrachten die nächsten Wochen damit, ihre Darbietungen zu üben und zu perfektionieren. Bella verbesserte ihre Mondsprünge, Max strickte schneller als je zuvor, Chester malte ein Meisterwerk, und Henrietta legte ihre glänzendsten goldenen Eier.

Der Tag des Großen Dorffests kam, und die Atmosphäre war von Aufregung erfüllt. Bauern aus der Nähe und Ferne hatten ihre besten Tiere mitgebracht, jeder hoffte, den großen Preis zu gewinnen. Der Festplatz war mit Ständen, Spielen und köstlichen Speisen gefüllt, und die Luft war erfüllt von Lachen und Musik.

Als es an der Reihe von Bauer Frank war, seine Tiere zu präsentieren, beobachtete die Menge gespannt. Bella begann mit ihren spektakulären Mondsprüngen, flog hoch in den Himmel und landete anmutig unter dem Jubel des Publikums. Max folgte, indem er in Rekordzeit eine riesige Decke strickte, seine behändigen Hufe arbeiteten wie Zauberei. Chester enthüllte dann sein Gemälde, eine atemberaubende Landschaft, die alle sprachlos machte. Schließlich betrat Henrietta die Bühne und legte ein goldenes Ei, das im Sonnenlicht funkelte.

Die Richter, darunter der angesehene Lord Pompington selbst, waren durchweg beeindruckt. Sie flüsterten miteinander, nickten und lächelten, während sie berieten. Schließlich stand Lord Pompington auf und verkündete: "Der Gewinner des Großen Dorffests und der Titel 'Bester Bauer des Landes' geht an keinen anderen als Bauer Frank und seine fantastischen Tiere!"

Die Menge brach in Applaus aus, und Franks Tiere sprangen und tanzten vor Freude. Frank strahlte vor Stolz, als er den großen Preis entgegennahm, und bedankte sich bei den Richtern und den Dorfbewohnern für ihre Unterstützung. Er wusste, dass nicht nur die Talente seiner Tiere den Tag gewonnen hatten, sondern auch die Liebe und Fürsorge, die sie alle teilten.

Von diesem Tag an wurde Bauernhof von Bauer Frank noch berühmter und zog Besucher aus der ganzen Welt an, die die magischen Tiere sehen wollten. Frank nutzte das Preisgeld, um den Hof zu verbessern und ihn zu einem noch besseren Ort für seine geliebten Tiere zu machen. Er baute einen neuen Stall für Bella, ein Strickstudio für Max, eine Galerie für Chester und ein goldenes Nest für Henrietta.

Aber das Beste daran war die noch stärker gewachsene Bindung zwischen Frank und seinen Tieren. Sie setzten die Dorfbewohner weiterhin mit ihren außergewöhnlichen Talenten in Staunen und Freude und ihre Freundschaft blühte von Tag zu Tag mehr auf. Zusammen zeigten sie, dass mit ein wenig Magie und viel Herz alles möglich ist.

Wally the Wonderful Whale

Once upon a time, in the vast and sparkling blue ocean, there lived a whale named Wally. Wally wasn't just any ordinary whale. He had the most brilliant, shimmering blue skin that seemed to sparkle like a thousand diamonds when the sun hit it just right. His size was impressive, even for a whale, and he had a heart as big as his body. Wally loved adventure, and he loved making new friends even more.

Every day, Wally would explore different parts of the ocean, meeting all sorts of sea creatures. There were Saffy the seahorse, who was the fastest swimmer in the sea; Oliver the octopus, who could juggle with all eight arms; and Mervin the manatee, who had the best jokes and could make anyone laugh. But Wally's best friend was Tilly the turtle, a wise and gentle soul who always knew the best stories and the safest paths in the ocean.

One sunny morning, Wally was swimming near the surface, singing his favorite sea shanty, when he noticed something unusual in the distance. It was a strange object, floating on the water. Curiosity piqued, Wally swam closer to investigate. As he got nearer, he saw that it was a boat, and on that boat was a little girl, looking very lost and very frightened.

Wally's heart went out to the girl. "Hello there!" he called out in his deep, booming voice. "What are you doing all alone out here?"

The girl jumped at the sound but then saw Wally's kind eyes and felt a bit reassured. "I'm Lucy," she said, her voice trembling a little. "I was on a boat trip with my family, but I got lost. I don't know how to get back to them."

Wally smiled, showing his big, friendly teeth. "Don't worry, Lucy. I'll help you find your family. Hop on my back, and we'll search the ocean together!"

Lucy hesitated for a moment but then climbed onto Wally's broad back. It was surprisingly comfortable, like sitting on a moving sofa. With Lucy safely aboard, Wally dove beneath the waves, his powerful tail propelling them through the water with ease.

They swam for hours, searching high and low, near coral reefs and deep underwater valleys, but there was no sign of Lucy's family. Lucy was starting to lose hope, but Wally kept her spirits up with his songs and stories about his adventures. He even introduced her to Saffy, Oliver, and Mervin, who all tried to help in the search.

Just when it seemed like they might never find Lucy's family, Tilly the turtle appeared, swimming gracefully towards them. "I've heard you're looking for Lucy's family," Tilly said with a wise smile. "I think I might know where they are."

Following Tilly's guidance, they swam to a quiet, hidden cove surrounded by tall, jagged rocks. There, anchored safely, was a boat that looked just like the one Lucy had described. As they approached, Lucy's eyes filled with tears of joy. "That's it! That's my family's boat!"

Wally and his friends watched as Lucy's parents, who had been frantically searching for her, spotted her and burst into relieved smiles. They waved and shouted with joy, and Lucy waved back, her face lit up with happiness.

With a gentle nudge, Wally helped Lucy back onto her family's boat. Her parents hugged her tightly, thanking Wally and his friends for their incredible help.

"We can't thank you enough, Wally," Lucy's mother said, her eyes shining with gratitude. "You're a true hero."

Wally blushed, which is quite a sight for a whale. "It was nothing," he said modestly. "I'm just glad Lucy is safe and back where she belongs."

As Lucy's family set sail to return home, Lucy called out to Wally, "I'll never forget you, Wally! Thank you for everything!"

Wally waved his fin and watched until the boat was just a speck on the horizon. He felt a warm glow of happiness inside, knowing he had made a difference.

Back in the ocean, Wally continued his adventures, exploring new places and meeting new friends. But he always kept an eye out for any other creatures in need of help, ready to lend a fin whenever he could.

And so, Wally the Wonderful Whale became a legend in the ocean, known far and wide not just for his sparkling skin and impressive size, but for his kind heart and his willingness to help those in need. He taught everyone that true greatness comes from the heart and that even the biggest creatures can make a difference with acts of kindness.

Wally der Wunderbare Wal

Es war einmal in den weiten und funkelnden blauen Ozeanen lebte ein Wal namens Wally. Wally war nicht einfach irgendein gewöhnlicher Wal. Er hatte die strahlendste, schimmernde blaue Haut, die wie tausend Diamanten funkelte, wenn die Sonne genau richtig darauf schien. Seine Größe war beeindruckend, selbst für einen Wal, und er hatte ein Herz so groß wie sein Körper. Wally liebte Abenteuer und noch mehr liebte er es, neue Freunde zu finden.

Jeden Tag würde Wally verschiedene Teile des Ozeans erkunden und allerlei Meereskreaturen treffen. Da waren Saffy, das Seepferdchen, das der schnellste Schwimmer im Meer war; Oliver, der Oktopus, der mit allen acht Armen jonglieren konnte; und Mervin, das Seekuh, der die besten Witze kannte und jeden zum Lachen bringen konnte. Aber Wallys beste Freundin war Tilly, die Schildkröte, eine weise und sanfte Seele, die immer die besten Geschichten und sichersten Pfade im Ozean kannte.

An einem sonnigen Morgen schwamm Wally nahe der Oberfläche und sang seine Lieblingsseemannslieder, als er in der Ferne etwas Ungewöhnliches bemerkte. Es war ein seltsames Objekt, das auf dem Wasser trieb. Neugierig schwamm Wally näher, um es genauer zu untersuchen. Als er näher kam, sah er, dass es ein Boot war, und auf diesem Boot war ein kleines Mädchen, das sehr verloren und sehr verängstigt aussah.

Wallys Herz ging zu dem Mädchen. "Hallo!" rief er mit seiner tiefen, dröhnenden Stimme. "Was machst du hier ganz alleine?"

Das Mädchen zuckte bei dem Klang zusammen, sah dann aber Wallys freundliche Augen und fühlte sich etwas beruhigt. "Ich bin Lucy", sagte sie, ihre Stimme zitterte ein wenig. "Ich war auf einem Bootsausflug mit meiner Familie, aber ich habe mich verirrt. Ich weiß nicht, wie ich zu ihnen zurückkehren soll."

Wally lächelte und zeigte seine großen, freundlichen Zähne. "Keine Sorge, Lucy. Ich werde dir helfen, deine Familie zu finden. Spring auf meinen Rücken, und wir werden zusammen den Ozean durchsuchen!"

Lucy zögerte einen Moment, kletterte dann aber auf Wallys breiten Rücken. Es war überraschend bequem, wie auf einem bewegten Sofa zu sitzen. Mit Lucy sicher an Bord tauchte Wally unter die Wellen, sein kräftiger Schwanz trieb sie mühelos durch das Wasser.

Sie schwammen stundenlang, suchten hoch und tief, in der Nähe von Korallenriffen und tiefen Unterwassertälern, aber es gab keine Spur von Lucys Familie. Lucy begann die Hoffnung zu verlieren, aber Wally hielt ihre Stimmung mit seinen Liedern und Geschichten über seine Abenteuer aufrecht. Er stellte sie sogar Saffy, Oliver und Mervin vor, die alle versuchten, bei der Suche zu helfen.

Gerade als es schien, als würden sie Lucys Familie nie finden, tauchte Tilly die Schildkröte auf, elegant auf sie zutreibend. "Ich habe gehört, dass du Lucys Familie suchst", sagte Tilly mit einem weisen Lächeln. "Ich glaube, ich weiß, wo sie sind."

Tillys Anleitung folgend, schwammen sie zu einer ruhigen, versteckten Bucht, die von hohen, zerklüfteten Felsen umgeben war. Dort, sicher verankert, war ein Boot, das genau wie das aussah, das Lucy beschrieben hatte. Als sie näher kamen, füllten sich Lucys Augen vor Freude mit Tränen. "Das ist es! Das ist das Boot meiner Familie!"

Wally und seine Freunde beobachteten, wie Lucys Eltern, die verzweifelt nach ihr gesucht hatten, sie entdeckten und erleichterte Lächeln aufsetzten. Sie winkten und jubelten vor Freude, und Lucy winkte zurück, ihr Gesicht strahlte vor Glück.

Mit einer sanften Berührung half Wally Lucy zurück auf das Boot ihrer Familie. Ihre Eltern umarmten sie fest und dankten Wally und seinen Freunden für ihre unglaubliche Hilfe.

"Wir können dir nicht genug danken, Wally", sagte Lucys Mutter, ihre Augen glänzten vor Dankbarkeit. "Du bist ein wahrer Held."

Wally wurde rot, was für einen Wal ziemlich ungewöhnlich ist. "Es war nichts", sagte er bescheiden. "Ich bin einfach froh, dass Lucy sicher ist und wieder dort ist, wo sie hingehört."

Als Lucys Familie in See stach, um nach Hause zurückzukehren, rief Lucy Wally zu: "Ich werde dich nie vergessen, Wally! Danke für alles!"

Wally winkte mit seiner Flosse und sah zu, bis das Boot nur noch ein Punkt am Horizont war. Er fühlte eine warme Glut des Glücks in sich, wissend, dass er einen Unterschied gemacht hatte.

Zurück im Ozean setzte Wally seine Abenteuer fort, erkundete neue Orte und traf neue Freunde. Aber er behielt immer ein Auge für andere Kreaturen, die Hilfe brauchten, bereit, eine Flosse zu leihen, wann immer er konnte.

Und so wurde Wally der Wunderbare Wal zur Legende im Ozean, weit bekannt nicht nur für seine funkelnde Haut und beeindruckende Größe, sondern für sein gutes Herz und seine Bereitschaft, denen zu helfen, die Hilfe brauchen. Er lehrte jeden, dass wahre Größe vom Herzen kommt und dass selbst die größten Kreaturen mit Akten der Güte einen Unterschied machen können.

Milly and the Marvelous Moon

Once upon a time, in a cozy little village nestled between rolling hills and lush meadows, there lived a curious girl named Milly. Milly had big, bright eyes that sparkled like stars, and she had a heart full of wonder and imagination. Every night, Milly would gaze up at the sky, fascinated by the twinkling stars and the glowing moon.

Milly loved to listen to stories about the moon, told by her grandmother, who was the village's best storyteller. Her grandmother would weave tales of magical adventures and mysterious creatures that lived on the moon, capturing Milly's imagination and filling her dreams with wonder.

One evening, as Milly sat outside, watching the moon rise above the horizon, she felt a strange tingling sensation in the air. The moon seemed to shimmer and glow brighter than usual, casting a soft, silvery light over the village.

Milly's curiosity was piqued. She decided to follow the moonlight, which led her to the edge of the village, where a shimmering pathway appeared, leading up into the night sky. Without hesitation, Milly began to climb the pathway, her heart pounding with excitement.

As she climbed higher and higher, the air around her grew cooler, and the stars seemed to twinkle with delight. Milly felt as if she was being drawn towards something magical, something extraordinary.

Finally, she reached the top of the pathway and stepped onto the surface of the moon. She gasped in amazement as she looked around, taking in the breathtaking landscape spread out before her. Craters dotted the surface of the moon, and in the distance, Milly could see mountains rising up into the sky.

But what truly took her breath away was the sight of the moon's inhabitants – a group of friendly, playful moon creatures, with sparkling eyes and shimmering fur. They welcomed Milly with open arms, inviting her to join them in their joyful games and dances.

Milly laughed and danced with the moon creatures, feeling as if she belonged among them. They showed her their favorite spots on the moon – the crystal-clear lakes where they liked to swim, the fields of moonflowers that bloomed only at night, and the secret caves filled with glowing crystals.

As the night wore on, Milly realized that she had lost track of time. She knew she had to return home before her family began to worry, but she couldn't bear to leave the marvelous moon and its enchanting inhabitants.

Just as she was about to say goodbye, the moon creatures gathered around her, their eyes shining with sadness. "Please don't go, Milly," they pleaded. "We've never had a visitor like you before. You bring so much joy and light to our home."

Milly's heart ached with longing, but she knew she had to return to her family. "I promise I'll come back," she said, tears welling up in her eyes. "I'll never forget this magical night, or the friends I've made here on the moon."

With a heavy heart, Milly climbed back down the shimmering pathway, her mind filled with memories of her incredible adventure. As she stepped back onto the familiar ground of her village, she looked up at the moon, shining brightly in the sky, and smiled.

From that night on, Milly would always look up at the moon with a sense of wonder and gratitude, knowing that somewhere up there, among the stars, her friends on the moon were watching over her, waiting for the day when she would return to their marvelous home.

Milly und der Wunderbare Mond

Es war einmal in einem gemütlichen kleinen Dorf, das zwischen sanften Hügeln und üppigen Wiesen eingebettet war, lebte ein neugieriges Mädchen namens Milly. Milly hatte große, leuchtende Augen, die wie Sterne funkelten, und sie hatte ein Herz voller Staunen und Fantasie. Jede Nacht würde Milly zum Himmel emporblicken, fasziniert von den funkelnden Sternen und dem leuchtenden Mond.

Milly liebte es, Geschichten über den Mond zu hören, die ihre Großmutter, die beste Geschichtenerzählerin des Dorfes, erzählte. Ihre Großmutter webte Geschichten von magischen Abenteuern und geheimnisvollen Kreaturen, die auf dem Mond lebten, und fesselte Millys Fantasie, füllte ihre Träume mit Staunen.

An einem Abend, als Milly draußen saß und den Mond über dem Horizont aufsteigen sah, spürte sie eine seltsame prickelnde Sensation in der Luft. Der Mond schien zu schimmern und heller als gewöhnlich zu leuchten, und warf ein weiches, silbernes Licht über das Dorf.

Millys Neugierde wurde geweckt. Sie beschloss, dem Mondlicht zu folgen, das sie zum Rand des Dorfes führte, wo ein schimmernder Pfad erschien, der in den Nachthimmel führte. Ohne zu zögern, begann Milly den Pfad hinaufzuklettern, ihr Herz pochte vor Aufregung.

Als sie höher und höher kletterte, wurde die Luft um sie herum kühler, und die Sterne schienen vor Freude zu funkeln. Milly hatte das Gefühl, dass sie zu etwas Magischem, zu etwas Außergewöhnlichem hingezogen wurde.

Schließlich erreichte sie das Ende des Pfades und betrat die Oberfläche des Mondes. Sie keuchte vor Erstaunen, als sie sich umsah und die atemberaubende Landschaft vor ihr aufnahm. Krater zierten die Oberfläche des Mondes, und in der Ferne konnte Milly Berge sehen, die in den Himmel ragten.

Aber was sie wirklich sprachlos machte, war der Anblick der Bewohner des Mondes - eine Gruppe freundlicher, verspielter Mondkreaturen, mit funkelnden Augen und schimmerndem Fell. Sie begrüßten Milly mit offenen Armen und luden sie ein, sich ihren fröhlichen Spielen und Tänzen anzuschließen.

Milly lachte und tanzte mit den Mondkreaturen, fühlte sich, als gehöre sie zu ihnen. Sie zeigten ihr ihre Lieblingsorte auf dem Mond - die kristallklaren Seen, in denen sie gerne schwammen, die Felder von Mondblumen, die nur nachts blühten, und die geheimen Höhlen, die mit leuchtenden Kristallen gefüllt waren.

Als die Nacht fortschritt, realisierte Milly, dass sie die Zeit aus den Augen verloren hatte. Sie wusste, dass sie nach Hause zurückkehren musste, bevor ihre Familie sich Sorgen machte, aber sie konnte es nicht ertragen, den wunderbaren Mond und seine bezaubernden Bewohner zu verlassen.

Gerade als sie Abschied nehmen wollte, versammelten sich die Mondkreaturen um sie, ihre Augen leuchteten vor Traurigkeit. "Bitte geh nicht, Milly", flehten sie. "Wir hatten noch nie einen

Besucher wie dich. Du bringst so viel Freude und Licht in unser Zuhause."

Millys Herz schmerzte vor Sehnsucht, aber sie wusste, dass sie zu ihrer Familie zurückkehren musste. "Ich verspreche, ich werde zurückkommen", sagte sie, Tränen stiegen ihr in die Augen. "Ich werde diese magische Nacht nie vergessen oder die Freunde, die ich hier auf dem Mond gefunden habe."

Mit einem schweren Herzen stieg Milly den schimmernden Pfad hinunter, ihr Kopf voller Erinnerungen an ihr unglaubliches Abenteuer. Als sie wieder festen Boden unter den Füßen hatte, sah sie zum vertrauten Himmel ihres Dorfes hinauf, in dem der Mond hell leuchtete, und lächelte.

Von dieser Nacht an würde Milly immer mit einem Gefühl des Staunens und der Dankbarkeit zum Mond aufblicken, wissend, dass irgendwo dort oben, zwischen den Sternen, ihre Freunde auf dem Mond über sie wachten und auf den Tag warteten, an dem sie in ihr wunderbares Zuhause zurückkehren würde.

The Gentle Giant of Meadowville

In a quaint village called Meadowville, nestled between green rolling hills and sparkling rivers, lived a giant named Gregory. Gregory was no ordinary giant. He was the kindest, most gentle soul anyone could ever meet. Standing at over twenty feet tall, with hair the color of autumn leaves and eyes as blue as the summer sky, Gregory was a sight to behold. Despite his enormous size, he had a heart as soft as a marshmallow.

Gregory's home was on the edge of Meadowville, in a cozy cave adorned with colorful flowers and twinkling fairy lights. The villagers were initially scared of Gregory because, well, giants were supposed to be scary, right? But Gregory soon won them over with his kind acts and warm smile.

One sunny morning, as Gregory was tending to his giant-sized garden, he heard a commotion coming from the village square. Curiosity piqued, he decided to see what was going on. With his long strides, it took Gregory no time at all to reach the center of Meadowville. There, he found a crowd gathered around a tall, thin man dressed in a shiny, colorful outfit. The man was standing on a wooden box, waving his arms dramatically.

"Ladies and gentlemen, boys and girls, I am Professor Pumpernickel, the greatest magician in the land!" the man announced. "I have come to Meadowville to present my incredible show of magic and wonder. But first, I need a volunteer."

The children in the crowd were excited, jumping up and down, eager to be chosen. But Professor Pumpernickel's eyes landed on Gregory. "How about you, my giant friend?" he said with a mischievous grin.

Gregory was taken aback. He had never been part of a magic show before. But seeing the eager faces of the children, he couldn't say no. "Alright," Gregory agreed, smiling shyly.

Professor Pumpernickel led Gregory to the center of the stage. "Ladies and gentlemen, I will make this giant disappear!" he declared. The crowd gasped in astonishment.

The magician began waving his wand, chanting mysterious words. Gregory closed his eyes, feeling a strange sensation wash over him. Suddenly, there was a loud pop, and when Gregory opened his eyes, he found himself in a dark, unfamiliar place. He looked around, confused. Where was he?

As his eyes adjusted to the darkness, Gregory realized he was inside a large, dusty attic. Cobwebs hung from the ceiling, and old furniture was scattered around. He tried to move but found himself trapped in a large, enchanted cage. Gregory's heart sank. He had been tricked!

Meanwhile, back in Meadowville, the villagers were growing anxious. "Where's Gregory?" they murmured. "What has happened to our gentle giant?"

Little did they know that Professor Pumpernickel was not a real magician, but a clever trickster who captured magical creatures and sold them to the highest bidder. He had used his "magic" to teleport Gregory into his secret attic, far away from the village.

Determined to escape, Gregory used all his strength to break the bars of the cage, but it was no use. The cage was enchanted with powerful spells. Gregory felt a wave of despair wash over him. He missed his home, his garden, and most of all, his friends in Meadowville.

Just as Gregory was about to give up hope, he heard a faint rustling sound. Out of the shadows emerged a small, scruffy cat with bright green eyes. "Hello there," the cat said, surprising Gregory. "My name is Whiskers. I've been trapped here for weeks. Who are you?"

Gregory explained his predicament, and Whiskers listened intently. "We need to work together to escape," Whiskers said. "I may be small, but I'm very clever."

With Whiskers' help, Gregory learned about the weaknesses in the enchantments that held him captive. Whiskers had discovered that the cage's magic weakened every night at midnight, just for a few minutes. It wasn't much time, but it might be enough.

That night, as the clock struck twelve, Gregory and Whiskers sprang into action. Gregory pushed against the weakened bars with all his might, and to his delight, they began to bend. Whiskers squeezed through the gap and helped Gregory push further until the bars gave way, and Gregory was free!

But their escape wasn't over yet. They had to find a way out of the attic and avoid Professor Pumpernickel. Using his giant ears, Gregory listened for any sounds. They heard the professor snoring loudly in the room below. Quietly, Gregory and Whiskers crept down the stairs and out into the cool night air.

Free at last, Gregory and Whiskers made their way back to Meadowville. The journey was long, but they encouraged each other along the way. When they finally arrived, the villagers were overjoyed. "Gregory! You're back!" they cried.

Gregory told them about Professor Pumpernickel's deception and how Whiskers had helped him escape. The villagers were furious. They decided to go to the nearby towns to warn them about the trickster magician.

As for Gregory, he was welcomed back with open arms. Whiskers became a permanent resident of Meadowville, living happily with Gregory in his cozy cave. The two friends were inseparable, sharing many more adventures together.

From that day on, the villagers of Meadowville learned never to judge someone by their appearance. Gregory, the gentle giant, was a beloved hero, and Whiskers, the clever cat, was celebrated for his bravery. Together, they showed that even the unlikeliest of friends could accomplish great things when they worked together.

And so, the gentle giant and his furry friend lived happily ever after, reminding everyone that kindness and courage could overcome even the trickiest of situations.

Der Sanfte Riese von Wiesental

In einem malerischen Dorf namens Wiesental, das zwischen grünen Hügeln und funkelnden Flüssen eingebettet war, lebte ein Riese namens Gregor. Gregor war kein gewöhnlicher Riese. Er war die freundlichste und sanfteste Seele, die man sich vorstellen konnte. Mit über sechs Metern Höhe, Haaren in der Farbe der Herbstblätter und Augen so blau wie der Sommerhimmel, war Gregor ein Anblick, der beeindruckte. Trotz seiner enormen Größe hatte er ein Herz, das so weich war wie ein Marshmallow.

Gregors Zuhause lag am Rande von Wiesental, in einer gemütlichen Höhle, die mit bunten Blumen und funkelnden Feenlichtern geschmückt war. Anfangs hatten die Dorfbewohner Angst vor Gregor, denn Riesen sollten doch furchterregend sein, oder? Aber Gregor gewann sie schnell durch seine freundlichen Taten und sein warmes Lächeln für sich.

Eines sonnigen Morgens, als Gregor seinen riesigen Garten pflegte, hörte er einen Tumult aus dem Dorfplatz. Neugierig geworden, beschloss er, nachzusehen, was los war. Mit seinen langen Schritten erreichte Gregor in kürzester Zeit das Zentrum von Wiesental. Dort fand er eine Menge, die sich um einen hochgewachsenen, dünnen Mann in einem glänzenden, bunten Anzug versammelt hatte. Der Mann stand auf einer Holzkiste und wedelte dramatisch mit den Armen.

"Meine Damen und Herren, Jungen und Mädchen, ich bin Professor Pumpernickel, der größte Magier im Land!" verkündete der Mann. "Ich bin nach Wiesental gekommen, um meine unglaubliche Show voller Magie und Wunder zu präsentieren. Aber zuerst brauche ich einen Freiwilligen."

Die Kinder in der Menge waren aufgeregt, hüpften auf und ab und hofften, ausgewählt zu werden. Aber Professor Pumpernickels Augen landeten auf Gregor. "Wie wäre es mit dir, mein riesiger Freund?" sagte er mit einem schelmischen Grinsen.

Gregor war überrascht. Er war noch nie Teil einer Zaubershow gewesen. Aber als er die erwartungsvollen Gesichter der Kinder sah, konnte er nicht Nein sagen. "In Ordnung," stimmte Gregor schüchtern zu und lächelte.

Professor Pumpernickel führte Gregor zur Mitte der Bühne. "Meine Damen und Herren, ich werde diesen Riesen verschwinden lassen!" erklärte er. Die Menge schnappte erstaunt nach Luft.

Der Magier begann mit seinem Zauberstab zu wedeln und geheimnisvolle Worte zu murmeln. Gregor schloss die Augen und spürte, wie ein seltsames Gefühl über ihn kam. Plötzlich gab es ein lautes Ploppen, und als Gregor die Augen öffnete, fand er sich an einem dunklen, unbekannten Ort wieder. Er schaute sich verwirrt um. Wo war er?

Als sich seine Augen an die Dunkelheit gewöhnten, erkannte Gregor, dass er in einem großen, staubigen Dachboden war. Spinnweben hingen von der Decke, und alte Möbel standen herum. Er versuchte sich zu bewegen, stellte aber fest, dass er in einem großen, verzauberten Käfig gefangen war. Gregors Herz sank. Er war hereingelegt worden!

Währenddessen wurden die Dorfbewohner in Wiesental zunehmend ängstlicher. "Wo ist Gregor?" murmelten sie. "Was ist mit unserem sanften Riesen passiert?"

Was sie nicht wussten, war, dass Professor Pumpernickel kein echter Magier war, sondern ein geschickter Betrüger, der magische Kreaturen einfing und an den Meistbietenden verkaufte. Er hatte seine "Magie" benutzt, um Gregor in seinen geheimen Dachboden weit entfernt vom Dorf zu teleportieren.

Entschlossen zu entkommen, nutzte Gregor all seine Kraft, um die Stäbe des Käfigs zu zerbrechen, aber es war vergebens. Der Käfig war mit mächtigen Zaubern verzaubert. Gregor fühlte, wie eine Welle der Verzweiflung über ihn hereinbrach. Er vermisste sein Zuhause, seinen Garten und vor allem seine Freunde in Wiesental.

Gerade als Gregor die Hoffnung aufgeben wollte, hörte er ein leises Rascheln. Aus den Schatten trat eine kleine, zottelige Katze mit leuchtend grünen Augen. "Hallo," sagte die Katze und überraschte Gregor. "Mein Name ist Whiskers. Ich bin hier seit Wochen gefangen. Wer bist du?"

Gregor erklärte seine Situation, und Whiskers hörte aufmerksam zu. "Wir müssen zusammenarbeiten, um zu entkommen," sagte Whiskers. "Ich bin vielleicht klein, aber ich bin sehr clever."

Mit Whiskers' Hilfe erfuhr Gregor von den Schwachstellen der Zauber, die ihn gefangen hielten. Whiskers hatte entdeckt, dass die Magie des Käfigs jede Nacht um Mitternacht für einige Minuten schwächer wurde. Es war nicht viel Zeit, aber es könnte genug sein.

In dieser Nacht, als die Uhr Mitternacht schlug, machten sich Gregor und Whiskers an die Arbeit. Gregor drückte mit aller Macht gegen die geschwächten Stäbe, und zu seiner Freude begannen sie sich zu biegen. Whiskers schlüpfte durch die Lücke und half Gregor weiterzudrücken, bis die Stäbe nachgaben und Gregor frei war!

Aber ihre Flucht war noch nicht vorbei. Sie mussten einen Weg aus dem Dachboden finden und Professor Pumpernickel vermeiden. Mit seinen riesigen Ohren lauschte Gregor auf Geräusche. Sie hörten den Professor laut im Raum darunter schnarchen. Vorsichtig schlichen Gregor und Whiskers die Treppe hinunter und hinaus in die kühle Nachtluft.

Endlich frei, machten sich Gregor und Whiskers auf den Weg zurück nach Wiesental. Die Reise war lang, aber sie ermutigten sich gegenseitig. Als sie schließlich ankamen, waren die Dorfbewohner überglücklich. "Gregor! Du bist zurück!" riefen sie.

Gregor erzählte ihnen von Professor Pumpernickels Täuschung und wie Whiskers ihm bei der Flucht geholfen hatte. Die Dorfbewohner waren wütend. Sie beschlossen, in die nahegelegenen Städte zu gehen und sie vor dem Betrüger zu warnen.

Gregor wurde mit offenen Armen empfangen. Whiskers wurde ein permanenter Bewohner von Wiesental und lebte glücklich mit Gregor in seiner gemütlichen Höhle. Die beiden Freunde waren unzertrennlich und erlebten viele weitere Abenteuer zusammen.

Von diesem Tag an lernten die Dorfbewohner von Wiesental, niemals jemanden nach seinem Aussehen zu beurteilen. Gregor, der sanfte Riese, war ein geliebter Held, und Whiskers, die clevere Katze, wurde für ihren Mut gefeiert. Gemeinsam zeigten sie, dass sogar die unwahrscheinlichsten Freunde Großes erreichen können, wenn sie zusammenarbeiten.

Und so lebten der sanfte Riese und sein pelziger Freund glücklich bis ans Ende ihrer Tage und erinnerten alle daran, dass Freundlichkeit und Mut sogar die kniffligsten Situationen überwinden können.

The Magical Piano and the Incredible Adventure

In a quaint village called Melody Town, there lived a boy named Theo. Theo was an ordinary boy with an extraordinary love for music. His room was filled with various musical instruments, but his favorite was an old, slightly dusty piano that had been in his family for generations. The piano had intricate carvings and a glossy finish that shimmered even in the dimmest light.

One rainy afternoon, as Theo sat playing a simple tune, he noticed something strange. The piano keys began to glow with a soft, golden light. The melody he was playing seemed to take on a life of its own, filling the room with a warm, magical aura. Startled but curious, Theo continued to play, his fingers dancing across the keys.

Suddenly, the piano emitted a brilliant flash of light, and before Theo knew it, he was no longer in his room. He found himself in a magnificent hall, filled with grand pianos, each more beautiful than the last. The hall was bathed in a gentle, golden glow, and the air was filled with the sweet sound of music.

"Welcome, Theo," a melodious voice called out. Theo turned to see a tall, elegant figure dressed in shimmering robes. "I am Harmonia, the Guardian of the Magical Piano."

Theo's eyes widened in amazement. "Magical piano?" he repeated.

Harmonia nodded. "Yes, this piano has the power to transport those who play it into the Realm of Music. Here, music comes to life in the most extraordinary ways. But be warned, Theo, this realm is filled with challenges that only the bravest and most talented can overcome."

Theo felt a mix of excitement and apprehension. "What kind of challenges?"

Harmonia smiled gently. "You must embark on a journey through the different musical lands. In each land, you will face a challenge that tests your musical abilities and your heart. If you succeed, you will be granted a magical note. Collect all the notes, and you will unlock the true power of the magical piano."

With a sense of determination, Theo agreed to the quest. Harmonia waved her hand, and a path of shimmering musical notes appeared before Theo's feet. "Follow the path, and let the music guide you," she said.

Theo set off on his adventure, his heart pounding with anticipation. The first land he arrived in was the Land of Rhythm. The ground beneath his feet pulsed with a steady beat, and the trees swayed in time to the music. Theo encountered a group of lively drum-playing creatures called Beatniks.

"To earn the first magical note, you must keep up with our rhythm," the leader of the Beatniks challenged. They began to play a complex, fast-paced rhythm on their drums.

Theo took a deep breath, closed his eyes, and let the rhythm flow through him. He tapped his feet and clapped his hands, matching the Beatniks beat for beat. The creatures nodded in approval, and with a final flourish, they handed Theo a glowing, golden note.

"Congratulations, Theo," the leader said. "You have passed the test of rhythm."

With the first magical note in hand, Theo continued his journey. The next land he entered was the Land of Melody. The air was filled with enchanting tunes, and flowers that looked like musical notes bloomed all around. Theo met a graceful bird named Lyra, who sang the most beautiful melodies he had ever heard.

"To earn the second magical note, you must create a melody that touches the heart," Lyra instructed.

Theo sat down on a rock and began to play a tune on his small, portable keyboard. He poured all his emotions into the music, thinking of his family, his friends, and his love for music. The melody that emerged was tender and heartfelt, bringing tears to Lyra's eyes.

"Such a beautiful melody," Lyra said, handing Theo the second magical note. "You have passed the test of melody."

Feeling more confident, Theo ventured into the next land, the Land of Harmony. Here, the trees sang in perfect harmony, and the rivers hummed gentle tunes. Theo met a wise old owl named Orpheus, who was an expert in harmonies.

"To earn the third magical note, you must harmonize with the natural world," Orpheus said.

Theo listened carefully to the sounds around him—the rustling leaves, the flowing water, the chirping birds. He began to play a harmony that blended perfectly with the natural symphony. Orpheus nodded in approval and gave Theo the third magical note.

"Your harmony is flawless, young one," Orpheus praised. "You have passed the test of harmony."

With three magical notes in hand, Theo felt a sense of accomplishment. But he knew there were more challenges ahead. The next land he arrived in was the Land of Tempo. Everything here moved at varying speeds, from the fast-paced winds to the slow, deliberate movements of the creatures.

Theo met a lively fox named Allegro, who was always in a hurry. "To earn the fourth magical note, you must master the changes in tempo," Allegro said, darting around energetically.

Theo played a piece on his keyboard, starting with a slow, steady tempo and gradually increasing the speed until it matched Allegro's quick movements. Then, he slowed it down again, demonstrating his control over the tempo. Allegro was impressed and awarded Theo the fourth magical note.

"You have a great sense of tempo," Allegro said. "You have passed the test of tempo."

With four magical notes, Theo moved on to the final land, the Land of Dynamics. Here, the music was powerful and emotional, ranging from soft whispers to thunderous roars. Theo met a majestic lion named Forte, whose roar could shake the ground.

"To earn the final magical note, you must show mastery over dynamics," Forte said, his voice booming.

Theo played a piece that showcased a wide range of dynamics, from gentle, quiet passages to loud, powerful crescendos. Forte nodded in approval and gave Theo the fifth magical note.

"You have a true understanding of dynamics," Forte said. "You have passed the test of dynamics."

With all five magical notes, Theo returned to the grand hall where Harmonia awaited him. "You have done it, Theo," she said with pride. "You have proven yourself a true master of music."

Theo placed the five magical notes on the piano, and they merged into a single, radiant note. The piano glowed with a brilliant light, and Theo felt a surge of power within him. He knew that this was the true power of the magical piano—the ability to touch hearts and bring joy through music.

"Thank you, Harmonia," Theo said. "This has been an incredible adventure."

Harmonia smiled. "Remember, Theo, the magic of music lies within you. Use it to bring happiness and light to the world."

With a final flash of light, Theo found himself back in his room, sitting at the piano. The golden glow had faded, but the memories of his adventure remained vivid. He began to play a beautiful melody, and as the music filled the room, he knew that the magic of the piano would always be with him.

And so, Theo continued to share his love of music with the people of Melody Town, touching hearts and bringing joy wherever he went. The story of Theo and the magical piano became a legend, inspiring everyone to believe in the magic of music and the power of dreams.

Das Magische Klavier und das Unglaubliche Abenteuer

Es war einmal in einem malerischen Dorf namens Melodienstadt, da lebte ein Junge namens Theo. Theo war ein gewöhnlicher Junge mit einer außergewöhnlichen Liebe zur Musik. Sein Zimmer war voller Musikinstrumente, aber sein Lieblingsinstrument war ein altes, leicht verstaubtes Klavier, das seit Generationen in seiner Familie war. Das Klavier hatte kunstvolle Schnitzereien und ein glänzendes Finish, das selbst im schwächsten Licht schimmerte.

Eines regnerischen Nachmittags, als Theo ein einfaches Lied spielte, bemerkte er etwas Seltsames. Die Klaviertasten begannen mit einem sanften, goldenen Licht zu leuchten. Die Melodie, die er spielte, schien ein Eigenleben zu entwickeln und erfüllte den Raum mit einer warmen, magischen Aura. Erstaunt, aber neugierig spielte Theo weiter, seine Finger tanzten über die Tasten.

Plötzlich strahlte das Klavier ein helles Licht aus, und bevor Theo sich versah, war er nicht mehr in seinem Zimmer. Er befand sich in einer prächtigen Halle, gefüllt mit großen Klavieren, jedes schöner als das andere. Die Halle war in ein sanftes, goldenes Licht getaucht, und die Luft war erfüllt von süßen Klängen der Musik.

"Willkommen, Theo", rief eine melodische Stimme. Theo drehte sich um und sah eine große, elegante Gestalt in schimmernden

Gewändern. "Ich bin Harmonia, die Hüterin des magischen Klaviers."

Theos Augen weiteten sich vor Erstaunen. "Magisches Klavier?" wiederholte er.

Harmonia nickte. "Ja, dieses Klavier hat die Macht, diejenigen, die es spielen, ins Reich der Musik zu transportieren. Hier wird die Musik auf die außergewöhnlichste Weise lebendig. Aber sei gewarnt, Theo, dieses Reich ist voller Herausforderungen, die nur die Mutigsten und Begabtesten bestehen können."

Theo fühlte eine Mischung aus Aufregung und Beklemmung. "Welche Art von Herausforderungen?"

Harmonia lächelte sanft. "Du musst eine Reise durch die verschiedenen Musiklande unternehmen. In jedem Land wirst du einer Herausforderung begegnen, die dein musikalisches Können und dein Herz auf die Probe stellt. Wenn du erfolgreich bist, erhältst du eine magische Note. Sammle alle Noten, und du wirst die wahre Kraft des magischen Klaviers freisetzen."

Mit einem Gefühl der Entschlossenheit stimmte Theo der Aufgabe zu. Harmonia winkte mit der Hand, und ein Pfad aus schimmernden Noten erschien vor Theos Füßen. "Folge dem Pfad und lass die Musik dich führen", sagte sie.

Theo machte sich auf sein Abenteuer, sein Herz pochte vor Aufregung. Das erste Land, in dem er ankam, war das Land des Rhythmus. Der Boden unter seinen Füßen pulsierte im Takt, und die Bäume wiegten sich im Takt der Musik. Theo begegnete einer Gruppe lebhafter Trommelwesen namens Beatniks.

"Um die erste magische Note zu verdienen, musst du mit unserem Rhythmus mithalten", forderte der Anführer der Beatniks. Sie begannen, einen komplexen, schnellen Rhythmus auf ihren Trommeln zu spielen.

Theo atmete tief durch, schloss die Augen und ließ den Rhythmus durch sich fließen. Er klopfte mit den Füßen und klatschte in die Hände, den Beatniks Schlag für Schlag folgend. Die Kreaturen nickten zustimmend, und mit einem letzten Trommelwirbel überreichten sie Theo eine leuchtende, goldene Note.

"Herzlichen Glückwunsch, Theo", sagte der Anführer. "Du hast den Rhythmustest bestanden."

Mit der ersten magischen Note in der Hand setzte Theo seine Reise fort. Das nächste Land, in das er gelangte, war das Land der Melodie. Die Luft war erfüllt von bezaubernden Melodien, und Blumen, die wie Noten aussahen, blühten überall. Theo traf auf einen anmutigen Vogel namens Lyra, der die schönsten Melodien sang, die er je gehört hatte.

"Um die zweite magische Note zu verdienen, musst du eine Melodie erschaffen, die das Herz berührt", wies Lyra an.

Theo setzte sich auf einen Felsen und begann, eine Melodie auf seiner kleinen, tragbaren Tastatur zu spielen. Er legte all seine Emotionen in die Musik, dachte an seine Familie, seine Freunde und seine Liebe zur Musik. Die Melodie, die entstand, war zart und gefühlvoll und brachte Lyra zu Tränen.

"Eine so schöne Melodie", sagte Lyra und überreichte Theo die zweite magische Note. "Du hast den Melodietest bestanden."

Mit mehr Selbstvertrauen wagte sich Theo ins nächste Land, das Land der Harmonie. Hier sangen die Bäume in perfekter Harmonie, und die Flüsse summten sanfte Melodien. Theo traf auf eine weise alte Eule namens Orpheus, die ein Experte für Harmonien war.

"Um die dritte magische Note zu verdienen, musst du dich mit der natürlichen Welt harmonisieren", sagte Orpheus.

Theo hörte aufmerksam auf die Geräusche um sich herum – das Rascheln der Blätter, das Fließen des Wassers, das Zwitschern der Vögel. Er begann, eine Harmonie zu spielen, die perfekt mit der natürlichen Symphonie verschmolz. Orpheus nickte zustimmend und übergab Theo die dritte magische Note.

"Deine Harmonie ist makellos, junger Freund", lobte Orpheus. "Du hast den Harmonietest bestanden."

Mit drei magischen Noten in der Hand fühlte sich Theo erfüllt. Doch er wusste, dass noch weitere Herausforderungen vor ihm lagen. Das nächste Land, in das er gelangte, war das Land des Tempos. Hier bewegte sich alles in unterschiedlichen Geschwindigkeiten, von den schnell wehenden Winden bis zu den langsamen, bedächtigen Bewegungen der Kreaturen.

Theo traf auf einen lebhaften Fuchs namens Allegro, der immer in Eile war. "Um die vierte magische Note zu verdienen, musst du die Tempowechsel meistern", sagte Allegro, der energiegeladen herumlief.

Theo spielte ein Stück auf seiner Tastatur, beginnend mit einem langsamen, gleichmäßigen Tempo und allmählich beschleunigend, bis es Allegros schnellen Bewegungen entsprach. Dann verlangsamte er es wieder und demonstrierte seine Kontrolle über das Tempo. Allegro war beeindruckt und überreichte Theo die vierte magische Note.

"Du hast ein großartiges Gefühl für Tempo", sagte Allegro. "Du hast den Tempotest bestanden."

Mit vier magischen Noten zog Theo weiter ins letzte Land, das Land der Dynamik. Hier war die Musik kraftvoll und emotional, von sanften Flüstern bis zu donnernden Gebrüll. Theo traf auf einen majestätischen Löwen namens Forte, dessen Gebrüll den Boden erzittern ließ.

"Um die letzte magische Note zu verdienen, musst du dein Können in Dynamik zeigen", sagte Forte mit donnernder Stimme.

Theo spielte ein Stück, das eine breite Palette an Dynamik zeigte, von sanften, leisen Passagen bis zu lauten, kraftvollen Crescendos. Forte nickte zustimmend und überreichte Theo die fünfte magische Note.

"Du hast ein wahres Verständnis für Dynamik", sagte Forte. "Du hast den Dynamiktest bestanden."

Mit allen fünf magischen Noten kehrte Theo in die große Halle zurück, wo Harmonia auf ihn wartete. "Du hast es geschafft, Theo", sagte sie stolz. "Du hast dich als wahrer Meister der Musik erwiesen."

Theo legte die fünf magischen Noten auf das Klavier, und sie verschmolzen zu einer einzigen, strahlenden Note. Das Klavier leuchtete in einem brillanten Licht, und Theo fühlte eine Kraft in sich aufsteigen. Er wusste, dass dies die wahre Macht des magischen Klaviers war – die Fähigkeit, Herzen zu berühren und Freude durch Musik zu bringen.

"Danke, Harmonia", sagte Theo. "Das war ein unglaubliches Abenteuer."

Harmonia lächelte. "Denke daran, Theo, die Magie der Musik liegt in dir. Nutze sie, um Glück und Licht in die Welt zu bringen."

Mit einem letzten Lichtblitz fand sich Theo wieder in seinem Zimmer, am Klavier sitzend. Das goldene Leuchten war verblasst, aber die Erinnerungen an sein Abenteuer blieben lebendig. Er begann, eine schöne Melodie zu spielen, und während die Musik den Raum erfüllte, wusste er, dass die Magie des Klaviers immer bei ihm sein würde.

Und so setzte Theo seine Liebe zur Musik in Melodienstadt fort, berührte Herzen und brachte Freude, wohin er auch ging. Die Geschichte von Theo und dem magischen Klavier wurde eine Legende und inspirierte alle, an die Magie der Musik und die Kraft der Träume zu glauben.